Wide Eyes Publishing

www.wide-eyes-publishing.com

ISBN: 9781793210982

Cover art by Mariana Gella

whisperings of the wild and wilting

wide eyes
publishing

Grace with Accountability

Musings of Mediocrity

Rising in Pisces

Love Letters to Ancestors

Truth over Harmony

Dedicated

to twenty somethings

stuck

in the betweens.

Your pain is poetry.

Your joy is poetry.

One day there will be balance.

Foreword

I have this theory that as humans we are inspired by stories of change and metamorphosis. There's no greater symbol of this than the lowly crawling caterpillar that changes into a beautiful soaring butterfly. But there's a stage that happens in between that glorious transformation and even this symbolic creature hides itself away during that time. That's really where my story lives. Often times when we experience these in between stages we don't have the words for them so we stay silent, which causes us to suffer alone. I spent most of my twenties staying silent.

This year I decided, I no longer want to suffer alone so I decided to stop staying silent. In this book I've compiled thoughts, quotes, and poems from my journals which I've kept from the time I was twenty until thirty. On these pages are my inner most reflections as I've processed my childhood trauma. In these words, are affirmations which have served me as I've stepped into myself as a woman, who refuses to yield my power. Written here are family histories I've compiled through my journeys to reconnect with my ancestors. These poems represent the evolution of my poetic voice and my evolution as a young woman.

But mostly, this book is an ode to twenty somethings stuck in between things. My hope is that my story empowers others to share their stories. When we share, we make space for support, solidarity, and shared experiences. When we share we no longer suffer alone. That is why there is power in our collective voices.

grace with accountability

Whisperings of the Wild

I believe in

going full force

toward those things that frighten you

enough to make you

pause.

That

is the whisperings of the wild.

Wild like Flowers

Bold

When I was 4
I was kicked out of a ballet class
The instructor told my mom
I refused to listen
though I was talented
I'd learn all the moves
more quickly than her other pupils
I'd then refuse to follow along with group.
Instead, I'd go off to the other side of the room
and start to make up my own moves.
She felt this level of independence was
disobedient.
My mother agreed
and made me apologize,
though I didn't understand why I should be sorry.
This was my first lesson in learning to hide
a bold spirit that lived
deep inside.

Haunted

As a teen,
I grappled with the sins of my father,
the emotional absence of my mother,
and being a role model to my sister.
Often
Feeling lost
Deeply introspective
Conflicted
Reflecting
on the world
moving around me.
I learned to pretend
to move with it.
I learned to "live"
continuing to be bold.
But haunted by
bad decisions
and fueled with
resentment.

Dangerous

20 brought more
conflictions,
somewhat bold yet apologetic
haunted and resentful.
That tension mixed
with youth and beauty
was a deadly cocktail...
One that was in high demand
among boys and men
who loved to torture themselves
with things they couldn't have.
I made them all pay
for the one man who was supposed to
teach me how to avoid them.
I tortured myself too
with boys and men I could never fully love
because vulnerability
had proven to be much more dangerous
and deadly to me
than my beauty.

Wild

Some may say that at 30,
I'm learning to not apologize
for my wildness.
But in reality,
I'm unlearning the habit of apologizing
for my wildness.
It's been ingrained deeply since 4.
I've decided though
as I thought about what I want to be
when I grow up
that if I can
be anything,
I want to be
Wild.
Not wild like the wind.
Not wild like the wolves.
But wild like the flowers.
Innately in-tune with the earth,
ever evolving.

Through dirt and decay
always finding a way
to blossom
to bloom...

Virgo

When you are earth
you must protect your soil.
Many living breathing things
will
sprout, bloom, and decay.
Many living things
will
absorb your nutrients,
often times leaving you
deficient
of proper hydration.

If you're here for
healing, reflection, therapy
then send along a bill.
I'm drained.
I'm not some
obscure idea
tucked
3,000 miles away
from your reality.
I am not here to raise anyone.
I've already had to raise myself.

I'm also a living breathing thing.

Sailing - unedited

Two ships set out
only to encounter stormy weather.
One looked to mother nature
The other to the arms of her father

And she did a very brave thing
Life happened.
Fought the winds with a spirit of fear
Emerged on the other side
Beautifully weathered
But resilient and revered.

It was easy to lock myself away
Anticipating
Her adventures
Hesitating
My own
Constantly second guessing
the need for control
Stability overshadowing
a need to feel whole.

As kids, both
Hope/full
God fearing
innocently exploring

As women, I
Hopeless
Fearing God
Devil's plan alluring

A dove never able to fly
A star in its place shines
Her happiness
A glimmer
Hope I internal

Central District 1987

When my heart is heavy
with suffering,
I rationalize it away.

As though
my pain
can only be weighed.

As if
suffering
operates like crabs in a bucket.

But there's no winners
                    here nor there…

Little Girls Raised in Glass Shelters

Shattered glass lined the sidewalk.
Many times, granny told her
not to play outside with her shoes off.
She did it anyway.
She ran to her mother and father crying.
Once again they were gone, away.
Not in physical absence
Never knowing emotional presence…
They were plagued with
a disease.

Same as the dirty old man
you weren't allowed to see.
An illness which caused him
to drop his glass pipe
the broken shards lining the street.
Born from addiction and raised
obliviously, living disgraced.
Girls trying to make sense of things
which can't be explained.

Yet taking the time
to make people stop on the street,
beauty leaving them amazed.
Caught up
in a false meaning of life.
Impossible to comprehend what is "right."
Disregarding anyone who ever tried,
choosing to live in darkness
not believing yourself worthy of light.

You are,
worthy of hanging posters
for a missing man in shelters,
dishonored.
Worthy of carrying him
to his bed because the sickness
makes him too lazy to bother.
Worthy of believing that a boy
perpetuating this cycle
could help you find the man
you're missing,
a man you call your father.

Outside of a desolate house
embarrassed to go inside
and fearing what you'll find.
The boy ran into an accomplice,
a former partner in the crime.
For once in his life,
he did something good
as he told him that her uncle had been inside.
Life like addiction
has many coincidences.
Every man connected.
Every woman facing the consequences.
A dealer living with her crack addicted uncle
beginning to see
in a different sense.

                                        She
                          always saw that world
                            from different eyes.
                         She never forgot those
                            little pieces of glass.
                         Her mom deficient in
                  comforting her while she cried.
                         She could never forget,
                           but she had to accept
                losing many family and friends
                        to this type of existence.
                Something in her started to see
                 again through a different lens.

Because
one day
rolling along
with another lost child,
who picked up her man
to pull a jugg
while she sat in the backseat,
they pulled up to a man on the corner
clinging to himself as he stood.
They drove him
30 minutes
so he could return all the clothes
his mother bought
for his children.
For him to buy
30 dollars
worth of drugs
30
became a symbol of love…

Seeing her own father…
Her mind in disbelief.
Her mouth unable to speak.
She knew immediately
that his little girls
would have glass
stuck in their hearts.
Potentially the same scars
that you could still see
on her feet.

But also,
this man knew
her mother and her uncle
before shattered pieces of glass,
her father,
her boyfriend,
or her,
were even a thought
an ember
or a particle.

It was at that instant,
I knew…
I had to let all
the fathers,
uncles, brothers
sons, and lovers
Go.
Because in the end,
they had never showed
up
when I needed
and the glass in my heart
had turned sharp…

But I wouldn't let them
hold me
in that trauma
nor that bondage.
I reacted and I responded.
I got out.
Now I'm free
to be a little girl who plays in the street
without the worry
of always having shoes
to protect my feet.

She held out her hand
and offered me
what no man ever could…

- *Sisterhood*

Silent Soldier

A silent fighter
in quiet war
is far more dangerous
than any boisterous
thoughtless
manifestation
you have presented...
I sat here.
I listened.
The wild and the bad
brewing within
would probably surprise you.

Irene

Your lust may plant a seed in the garden of her admiration
which will water itself with purity as it grows strong with her adoration.

Genuine at first you'll seem, as the fan blows, given time she will see that
you're not.
It only takes a second for a bite of an apple to turn brown as it sits and
rots.

Be careful of the women whose cocoons turn into fluttering wings of
butterflies
because that breeze lights the torch of resentment, which burns as they
discover your lies.

The winds will howl as that breeze grows powerful.
Your heart desires just to live with the warmth of the sun, blissful.

Safe to fall in the summer but summer turned now to fall.
Intentions revealed now the revenge of thunder's call.

Disappointment driving the speed. Oh, yes, a storm "is a-brewing."
Body language, rips through the city leaving everything behind it, in ruins.

He realizes, too late, the fate of his foundation destroyed with a natural yet
saintly wrath.
God counts her tears allowing her in the end to destroy everything in her
path.

She waited in vain,
actions resonate with the pain,
and she won't enable you to make another woman feel the same.

The original sin
lives on in the hearts of men
Hatred born from love. Women's hearts never fully able to mend.

Remember, she is a vehicle for life.
Nothing in humanity will suffice.
Through the divinity of forgiveness, you can learn to treat her right.

Be mindful of your deeds.
Pay attention to her needs.
Because often hurricanes stem from an apple's seed.

The sky and I
have been out of sync
lately.

Dark clouds roll in
around 5 p.m.
disrupting productivity.

Torrential downpours have been brewing
filling potholes quicker than I can
swim.

Alas, the mind gets carried away
by the absence of
light.

Spinning in disillusionment
is this all an elaborate
illusion?

"Woman, you've got a muse patiently waiting on your shoulder."

Ariel
Havana, Cuba
2018

Dreams Which Sit on the Chin
dedicated to Sandra Cisneros

In another life I've been...

A witch
with long dark hair and pink lips
who walks around in sable cotton capes
on Sundays
scaring the pure on the street
threatening in my presence
refusing to stop practicing my magic
standing firm in my beliefs.
Who worships the darkness
with such conviction
it makes preachers jealous
and ushers contemplate conversion.
A woman who is surrounded by
concrete developments
but only feels fulfilled by
natural elements
a fleshly yearning
that burns her at the stake.

In another life I've been...

An opera singer
with long dark hair and pink lips
who walks around in emerald silk gowns
on Wednesdays
to lounge around the house
refusing to talk to people
to not compromise my voice.
Who sings with such emotion
it makes grown men cry
and tired women stand
for ovations.
A woman who is surrounded by
fanatics and lovers
but filled with a loneliness
a sensual longing
that keeps all coming back.

In another life I've been...

A housewife
with long dark hair and pink lips
who walks around in rose chiffon blouses
on Saturdays
to clean the house
refusing to ask for help
for only I can truly get it right.
Who runs the household with such grace
it makes the children beam with adoration
and the husband bask in all her efficiency
though they show no appreciation.
A woman who is surrounded by
fake smiles and half truths
but finds a way to be resilient
with gentle apathy
that keeps them all in check.

I long to be
all the dreams
they sat on their chins...

Presents

You've been given the gift
of beauty they say
though it seems vain and selfish.

People feel entitled to gawk and gaze
as though it's some kind of
present.

Have you ever seen a toddler when
their new toy has been taken away?
Tantrums often turn violent.

I don't want to be pretty today but
they say
I don't own it.

I Am Not Maria

When we lock eyes,
I see her reflection
in the tears that he cries.
Her beauty,
indescribable.
He always seems to reminisce.
I can feel her when we kiss.
His Maria in the distance,
Elegant.
I hear her call his name
while we sleep at night.
And his grip becomes intense
as he clings to me tight.
I'm basking in him and therefore her…
I cringe; I binge
on his fears.
I listen; hope glistens
in his tears.
He can only see his sweet Maria
the woman who owns his soul.
I seek her out, pray for her demise,
though I know it won't make him whole.
I try to mimic her,
become her,
but I am not her.
I'd wash his dirty, bruised, tired feet with my own hair
as though our love is immaculate.
Though he'd never admit
he only sees Maria. Maria
unconditional
innocent.
But a man with only one wish
is not a man who
wishes to die content.
And the woman who prays to hold his heart
may be,
so you see
we are both
dangerous.

Inner Voice

What if self-doubt is self-debt
that we pay to our dreams?
What if our happiness
is hiding deep
in our uncertainty?

Retail

I am not here.

     I am everywhere.

     I am somewhere.

     I am nowhere.

But I am not here.

(In)visible Vessel

I am the only one who
has to stand in front of
a mirror
and be reminded that there is
a vehicle
which traps this soul
while shoes leave
imprints on concrete
where I stand
the vessel which has been
blamed
for crimes of the mind
at its best admired for
its strength
at its worst a victim,
criminalized
and words which cut the heart
deep inside
it's a wonder I can still stand before its reflection
planted fierce and grounded with
its feet
which carry through days
good and long
that leave thoughts racing
but still the body
struts along
if this thing is a manifestation
of what I hold inside
why
do I treat it like a prison
sometimes
instead of a glass case
protecting
a treasured prize

Pivotal Moment

I felt like a weight
sitting in a small room
thousands of miles away from
home
on Holborn street.
Windows wide open
but the air that trickled in
tasted of bitter relief.
Classmates moving pencils
furiously in unison as they
dissected Keats.

My stomach turned
over Keats' "urn"
and my face started to sting
because I'd never heard
of such a thing.
The pages underneath me
stained
with tears
the color of mahogany
skin.

A juxtaposition, a paradox.
Imposter syndrome
creeping in,
an unorthodox student
being charged with a felony
and uncertainty waiting back
home.
Feelings of inadequacy
paralyzing with silence.
The secrets I was keeping in,
heavy.

Each day, my colleagues
discussed the tensions
between "romanticism"
and "transcendentalism."
Grappling with their own
weighty presence
with confidence
that these words and ideas
belonged to them.
As I sat uncertain,

anger bit
at all the words
that sat on my tongue
refusing to leave my lips
and I envied them…
A self-advocacy
an agency
an opportunity
had been poured onto their
tongues
like honey since they were born.

I'd only tasted
this liberated tautness,
this slow sweetness,
grappling with self-actualization
for the first time at 15
over Hennessey,
which we poured onto the
streets
to mourn hood Socrates.
Who though wise would never
grow old
nor travel to such a foreign
place.

Wandering through concrete
columns,
exploring objects of our
argumentation,
I planted two feet
in front of that Grecian urn.
Pondering my existence,
igniting existential crisis,
I envisioned my childhood
a little girl surrounded by
emerald trees, mountains,
and gun violence.

That little girl
crossed an ocean alone
to stand in front of
an artifact
ancient, beautiful, and tangible.
The two hands which had
molded and shaped this display
lived centuries

before the idea of me
was even conceived.

Yet me in my Nikes and
the ten fingers of an ancient
sculptor
were connected in that moment.
A realization trickled down
cheeks
now staining the chest.
I stumbled upon something
profound
to better understand myself.
In that moment,
I was the poem and the urn,
limitless and infinite through
time and space.

That day, an internal revolution
sparked an affirmation
and a sense of belonging
formed.
As we debated, meter and
rhythm,
Thoreau and Emerson,
their relevance,
I found myself again
surrounded by trees and
mountains

with a bitter sweet disposition
of man-made things.
I began to connect with peers
beyond the difference
of mahogany skin,
and the life experiences
that were often in opposition
began to give me an advantage.
I felt at ease
having already pondered
philosophical questions on
existence
over hood theory, "the streets",
and pints of Hennessy.

You see, when we are amongst
ancient artifacts, leaves, and
trees
we can all finally find ourselves
as we were meant to be
bare,
supernatural,
and with new found serenity.
Immortalized in words,
limitless, infinite,
and that is the beauty
of poetry.

We fear change
even though we are one
with nature
and life's guarantee
is the coming and going
of seasons.

Embrace the change sis

Adventure

Ripples in the stream
gleam.

Seagulls surround and swarm
ready to descend.

Mocha skin beams and
glistens.

Floral kimono picks up waves and wind,
adventure commences.

Collections

As a girl I used to collect seashells.
I was taken with the sound of the ocean.
It was my first cognizance of the depth of the world.
As a woman I stand on the edge of you,
taken with all that is your being.
I take in the smell of your crisp and bitter wind.
I bask at the profundity of you.
I am daydreaming of fully submerging myself in you
and allowing myself to be swept away.
Yet I stand hesitantly on the edge,
paralyzed by your power.
The sound of you still calls me…
I'm stuck somewhere between the dangerous sounds of wave crashing
violently into rock.
And the serene sounds of waves sweetly and gently rippling with the
slightest tickling from the wind.
All happening simultaneously
in unison.
While I foolishly and yet staunchly stand
collecting moments.

musings of mediocrity

The Marsh

There's something about youth
that makes you unafraid
to wade
through the marsh.
Unknown terrain
and discoveries which in your
mind
can only be illuminating.
No fear of the things
undiscovered.
An arrogance, a restlessness,
which guides your untamed
heart
and no fear of death.

Reaching down
to catch tadpoles
without hesitation
for chipped red nail polish
or the lingering smell
of seaweed on your skin.
Observations of cranes
elegant
as they swoop to land
with outstretched limbs
in the soft dissolving sand.

Crabs clawing at air
quickly burrow themselves
as the vibrations
of your voice boom through the
ground.
Mosquitos lustful for new
flavors
they don't taste often
bite their way toward richness
from arms to ankles.
You shoo them away
without a care
for the itchy mounds that form
on your skin...
Because you're on a mission.

Rushing toward grass
which welcomes you
with a merciful breeze.
There's no fear for things
you can't initially see
because nothing feels
threatening.
Just quick moving calves
which hope to reach
the glittering sea,
and a mind which is
infatuated
with pondering how deep
the water might be
and a heart which
doesn't yet
fear the answer.

About a Boy...

Where dust settles on old books,
long forgotten.
Where dog ears hold pages,
profound statements.
Where spines have come undone…
Where illustrations have faded…
Provocative
yet antiquated.

Soul Food

peach cobbler

sonny rollins

greens

yams

grits (with cheese)

cocoa butter

kisses

sweet nothings

old bay

beauty marks

moonlight

The Wall

They built a wall for all to share,
and an anguished, despairing painter
decided to make it a beautiful thing
feeling its potential to assuage her grief.

She went to the wall each day
with canisters of spray paint
posting artwork of her experiences
and basking in a world without dissent.

But only the parts of her life she wanted to be seen.
Slowly people stopped their busy little feet
to offer their compliments
and she became the talk of the town.

As her *following* grew she became obsessed
and learned to anticipate their interest.
She started to paint the parts of her life they wanted to see…
Their affirmations had become one with her confidence.

Though repressive to her needs she obsessed
over the spots on her overalls and *filters* which strained the paint.
She attempted to compartmentalize the grief
smoothening the lines and enhancing the hues of her life.

She threw her dirty old apron out in the garbage.
Obsessing over whether passersby
would comment or like her without it
but also fearing silence as her worth's confirmation.

One day, she painted the inner desolation
that was her trauma and
no one even stopped to ask if
she was ok…

She took a bucket of white paint
and threw it on the mural of her pain
covering it up with a learned sense of false joy
while everyone stopped to pay it a compliment.

She yearned to return to a time
when the wall didn't exist in this place
and when she could sit cross legged
in the grass carefree to play.

No one here to wipe away her tears
or to tell her to pick up her chin.
Just *followers* disguised as friends,
scrolling by fast…

The Barren Landscape

I live in a place where

it doesn't

rain

where cleansing happens by chance

where succulents thrive but flowers

can't be

maintained.

A desolate place where children must be providers of

their own

nourishment

where healing seems unattainable

yet to sow such vibrant seeds

is divine

accomplishment.

What does it matter
if it rains
while you're
drowning?

-Malaise

A Something of Somethings

No energy for planning
said the cosmic dreamer.

No energy for drafting
said the practical teacher.

No energy for editing
said the devoted lover.

No energy for publishing
said the exhausted writer.

At times,
this
is a genre-less book
which
lacks an inspiring
protagonist.

Between You and Me

You cause laughter and frustration
in such tight spaces.
When I erupt, I'm not sure if it'll leave
delight
or destruction.

I Am

I am a teacher
without a lesson
filled with ignorance and questions.
Maybe
I am not a teacher
but
I am
a learner.

I am a partner
without a husband
seeking solace in empty companions.
Maybe
I am not a partner
but
I am
a lover.

I am a poet
without a poem
a blank empty rectangular canvas.
Maybe
I am not a poet
but
I am
an artist.

Gibbous

every time someone scoffs
at your
obsession with the moon
remind them
that if
the tension
between the
earth and it
can cause
entire bodies of water
to shift,
push and
pull,
rise and
fall
how could
it not have an effect
on
something so small?

if they insist
on numbers and science
remind the numerist
that your body
is 70% water
and
remind the atheist
that human beings
are nature too
and at the mercy
of its forces.

Dedicated to the boy who feels in flowers.

Generational Silence

The heat is heavy and thick
back East.
It sits weighing with a stench
that sticks to your skin, making you feel unclean.
Sweat beads
drip from the corner of your forehead
down to your mouth
and a week ago I would've laughed.
But today I'm quiet; I feel unclean.
Fruit sits in a basket from Target.
And though you spent hours killing gnats,
it's all in vain.
The plantains
(you would've thought) we neglected,
though strong and resilient,
have gone bad.
The clock ticks deafening in the silence,
heavy and thick with disappointment.
A droplet finally forms near brow
and slides down
tingling to Cupid's bow.
Stinging
with salt near a cut in my mouth,
wounded by silence.
I finally find my voice
in a harrowing gasp.

Hot Cheese and Grits

Hot Cheese and grits,
convenient and quick.

Hot cheese and grits,
don't let them sit.

On the stove waiting.
Walking around, you
anticipating…
Now that all is done, food's
ready
time to eat, everything
unsteady.

Be careful not to leave them on
too long
before they get hot
and start to pop.

Try not to leave too much
unsaid
we just got out of bed.
Breakfast wouldn't be the same
without this awkwardness and
shame.

I still have you in me…
After I had you
for the first time in me.

I finally found you and me.

All I want to do is make you a
plate
while we ignore fate.
Play a little while longer
let my feelings build stronger.

Escape reality.
Evade privacy.

Everyone knows
how to make hot cheese and
grits.
"It's never good for you," they
always say,
but we both eat them anyway.

Add a little bit of cheese to give
them some extra flavor.
Add a little bit of pepper spice
so your mouth can savor.

The simplicity
that is hot cheese and grits.
Still, the complexity
of you and I
sits.

Gratitude, Detachment

I have solace in being soot
burned brightly
burned to the ground
burned to protect seedlings.
I have solace in being dirt
trampled over
trampled on by feet
trampled nutrients packed tightly.
I have solace in being dust
forgotten embers
forgotten life remains
swept to new homes by wind

Love Letters to the Infinite Daydreamer

there's something
to be said
about a wish
as
it's whisked
away
by riotous winds,
unruly and undisciplined
carried off
into uncertainty
becoming one
with the
limitless
spirit of the universe
vibrating in its defense

Selenite

Sometimes you just
have to let things sit.

Walk away from them
for a bit
when you find yourself restless.

Come back when it feels right
you might find all you needed
was time
and clarity of mind.

Termination

A star in the sky,
tears well in my eyes.

A beautiful flower,
an intimate power.

Bonds severely torn,
life as you know it turned.

Sponsored by the state,
in a reality of self-hate.

Acting "out of love,"
she released a dove.

A man she resents.
A child cries upset.
A mother filled with regret.

The power of a bond
thoughtlessly severed from its mom.

An opportunity,
a life
gone.

Busy

I stopped moving
only for a moment
to realize
I hadn't sat with myself
in a while.
I went to the water
to listen to how gentle the breeze
tickled the waves.
All of a sudden wetness
kissed my cheek,
stinging.
The same place lips used to meet,
tingling.
Hitting me with
a revelation,
and then I remembered why
I had to stay
busy.

Sola Toda Sola

been having trouble slowing down
the worrying of people pleasing
lost myself in approvals and musings
the mania of multi-tasking

Cycles

I've searched for
boys and men
in trap houses
both dealers
and those itching to be healed.

I've searched for
men and boys
on desolate streets
both cold-blooded drug lord
and desperate fein.

I've searched for a man in boys who felt familiar.
I've searched for a man in boys who felt similar.

I hate the idea that being broken
is the only way to be built back up.

Though my trauma has made me resilient,
joy has always kept me going.

- *On Resilience*

For days
when all you do
is put out fires
ask yourself,
what would happen
if you just let the fire burn?
Fire often quells itself
and once the soot
starts to settle...
Peace.

let it burn sis

rising in pisces

Firefly,

I have the life we used to hope for in each other's arms by moonlight,
but my eyes once vibrant with honey are now a sorrowful sight.

In between the bustling of dreams once distant fantasy
are lingerings of broken promises and a space now empty.

When my pen hits paper with thoughts of you droplets still stain the page.

This is a memoir to the nostalgia and a testimony to my pain.

You Are Poetry

You don't call me friend,
but you won't call me lover.
This limbo leaves my heart torn between:
comfort
anxiety
excitement
depression
inspiration
frustration
but most often
confusion.
The in-between breeds belly aching laughter.
The in-between breeds eye aching puddles of tears.
Both send my pen to paper with fire and fury.

Éden

If I
let you
play
in my
garden…

Would you
water
my flowers?

Would you
tend to my
weeds?

Would you
shower me
with attention?

Would it
come to you
with ease?

Natural Phenomenon

Your hands softly run down my collar bone.
As I drink you up, you give me new energy.
You sense my eagerness and quench my appetite
with kisses,
nourishing the longing that intense desire can create.

Your lips press gently against mine,
and I turn into a pool, splashing with uncontrollable enthusiasm.
You restore my sexual consciousness and revitalize me
as your tongue
stimulates and dampness turns to saturation.

The warmth of your skin moves along my torso,
and I flow like a river, melting but exhilarated.
You travel downhill fueled with anticipation and ready to devour me
using hands
you release my appetite for lustful satisfaction.

Now your forefinger lingers as you part my thighs.
I'm fully immersed in the lake of your pleasure, revived.
You cover me with affection and embrace me with sensuality
your nose tickles
my flesh is unraveling with vulnerability.

Your essence is as exuberant as moonlight on my skin.
The full tide rises, waves of passion crash against my deepest fantasies.
I surge, I swell, undulating as you take me in wholly
the depth of you
the gravitational pull is a natural phenomenon.

Lips
gorging on my flower.

Tongue
forging its way to my nectar.

Drink to your satisfaction...
Devour me indulgently…

Flower Boy

The Terrace

She planted flowers
on his terrace
and every morning she watered them
with water from his sink
while every night she snuck out
to see if they were growing…

After many days like this
and no progress
one night she wept
over their barren soil
and in the morning little green sprouts
peaked their heads out
to console her.

Boundaries

Passive interest
doesn't resonate with my existence.

I'll swallow you whole
before I accept this type of distance.

Gemini

I want to raise you
and even though
I know
that's not love,
I can't help myself but to indulge.

Black Love

He was taught
that he had to be a man.
Sometime after he stopped
needing help
to get his shoes tied
and before
he lost his first tooth.

My lap was couch to his musings.
My shoulders were the alter for
him to surrender suffering
to diligent prayer warriors
convicted with his saving.

He appreciated
both my strength
and my stillness
the ability to
bear witness
to his struggles
but swallow my own
while he rationalized
that our burdens were the same.

A Hard Day's Work

He said he
needed closure
but I
have nothing left to say...
"How can you be both cane sugar
AND malt vinegar?"
He yelled spitefully.
"Why do you approach me
with such fire and fury
when I long
only
to water every single
dandelion in your garden?"
I sighed deeply....
"Say something, anything!"
He yelled desperately,
responding
to his own pleas.
I'm battling inside my head,
intently...
Wondering if he knows
how to let malt vinegar sit
because it requires patience
to cultivate such complex flavor.
Wondering how dandelions
will grow
if weeds are not pulled
deep from their roots.
I don't need a careless chef
preoccupied with convenience
nor a lazy caretaker
deceived by the flower's petals vibrance.
He said he
needed closure
but I
am a hard day's work..

Classical Element

Like air.
You were taken with my stillness.
My capacity to feel and be felt
absent of touch.
You took me in deep
exhaling all of your toxins
inhaling a freshness
that flowed right to your heart.
Sometimes my cool breeze could turn into a warm and chaotic wind.
You sought to harness it
but the pressure and sheer force frightened
and excited you simultaneously.
Wild
and non-conforming
just dangerous enough to be entertaining
Difficult to look away.

Like water.
I fed off of your reflection
of my own being
and everything I embodied.
Revealing myself anew in your eyes.
Reveling
We both bathed
And cleansed
Feeling new
Leaving a dark ring of desire.
But with the same force
that aroused your attention
the crashing waves of my ocean
soon turned into subtle droplets
running down my own freckled cheeks
Invisible
Purposefully hidden from you
For fear that the tension could betray my power.

Like Fire.

Wild
Passionate
impossible to contain.
Anger erupted and turned
destructive
Disastrous.
Developing slowly,
it consumed itself from inside out until there was nothing left inside me
but soot.
And where were you to be found?
You left me...
You left me to survey the damage.
You left me to question all of my elements.
The very existence which enticed you
and gave you life,
you left in rubble and ruin without explanation.
Unconcerned with the wreckage you left behind.

Like earth.

You are no match
for my Divine feminine energy.
Your words will never carry more meaning
than my intuition.
The vagueness of your intentions,
though it threw off my equilibrium,
will not keep me down for long.
My energy comes from my ancestors.
Their struggles,
their lessons are ingrained in my DNA.
My intuition from my mother
who is one with nature.
She cleanses, rebuilds, and destroys anything in her path.
Your intentions
are thoughtless, childish, selfish.
Fading into the aether as quickly as conception.
I am from the earth.
Bury me.
I will sprout roots.
I will reach to
the sun,
lift up my arms and rise.
I am from the earth.

Liberation

Truth is the epitome of liberty
for lovers
because it governs our action.
You denied me that right,
and yet
we met on battle lines
fighting simply for equity.
And now
you wonder why
there's fire on my tongue
when you've always known
freedom burns deep in my belly.

Narcissus

I loved a man
once
obsessed with his own
likeness.
He swore
I was his
goddess
of love,
the most beautiful
and only
ruler to his heart.
But I could tell
he loved only
the sparkle
in my eye
because of the glare
of his own
reflection.

More of Desires

You kissed me
like your lips would erupt
and catch fire
if the wetness
of my tongue
did not quell the flame
of your desire.

Live

He said he loved my undressed lips
The way my tongue sits
intimately near teeth...
The way it rolls over
pronunciations
and the images it brings...

"I'll let you worship me; only without expectations."

Pussy Monologues

Twice upon a Time

Twice upon a time,
I fell in love with you.
Once was bliss.
The latter was a miss.
We said last goodbyes
now twice,
and yet still
I ponder the if....

Perspective

I used to think I was the sun.
You were my fern.
When I realized I was the gardener,
I watered your roots with my tears.

Beware of lovers who try to rewrite history
when the war is over....

The Season of Instauration

his water wasn't entirely authentic

because he hadn't

honed his power yet

and to watch him grapple

with his destiny

spoke to something deep

inside me

cognitive spaces, youth was fleeing

sanguine places, optimism was fleeting

and I loved seeing him

in revolution

because at my core I'm an activist

but I made the assumption that

I would be

on the other side

when the dust settled

instead of watching him move forward

from behind enemy lines

now that I'm free

I'm on the fence

because I'm unsure if

I am a prisoner in his war

or if I am still fighting in his defense

Nostalgia

When your mouth belonged to me
I poured honey into it.

When your fingertips laid into me
I released all of my boundaries.

When your eyes commanded mine
I filled them with moon beams.

You live in sentimental longings.
The sweetest things are the most haunting.

Every time you resist letting the tears hit your chin
remember that you are mostly made of water
and even water can hold toxins.

Let that shit go sis

Firefly,

I've gone to war with myself to forget you
and lost every time.

I miss the way your words bounced off
hopeful places in my mind.

How they left my soul at a crossroads
with two paths undefined.

I miss the ambivalence of the unknown,
now standing on the other side.

love letters from ancestors

A Home Unknown

we take for granted our last names
being able to read and write them
the privilege it is
to our children
when
we become ancestors
and they journey to find us…

we take for granted our language
moving in and out of tongues
without accents that
our parents fought for us to lose
and yet we return to them
because
something deep in our bellies calls…

Wash Days

Mama used to sit me in her lap
on Sundays
for braids, twists, curls,
bobbles, ballies, barrettes, and rubber bands

she'd start with a cold wash
and kiss me on the tip of my forehead
as the water always seemed to run down my spine
and I'd giggle beaming up at her brown eyes

as I sat between her legs
squirming from the pulling and yanking
Mama would say, "stop child,
it don't hurt that bad," in only her way

we joked that if I flinched
Mama would "beat me with the comb"
though my hair was stubborn and my scalp tender,
Mama's hands were always as gentle as her heart

Sundays were for marathons of star trek
cuz Mama loved sci-fi (still does), she'd oohh and ahhh
as she massaged grease through my scalp
while I rolled my eyes but watched on

Sundays now are for nostalgia and wash days
as I take out the shampoo, conditioner, flexi rods, and coconut oil
put on an old t-shirt and turn on a marathon
I think of Mama…

The Soul of a Rebel

My mother is an elephant
regal and elegant
tranquil and serene.

My father a bull
tempered and prideful
stubborn and furious.

They fight incessantly
while their battles
imprison me.

I am constantly
in renaissance
in ruin
in revolution
longing to be free.

Decolonizing Curves Part I

I'm inspired by my curves because
my body has been the site of historical violence.
How could something so soft
so irrepressible
be the site of such violence.
Many grapple with ownership,
censorship;
While at the same time
lusting after companionship,
worship.
But I'm taking back
what has always been…
MINE.

Lá Rosa Negra

I've been called many things over the last century:
mixed
mulatta
morena
biracial
mestiça
multiracial
Pêro nunca blanca (never white)
y aveces negra (sometimes black)
gringa
chica
menina
americana
chingona
(my personal favorite).
While many ask,

"What are you?" or even "Where are you from?"

Most never ask me
how to pronounce my name.

I feel at home in so many places it's unsettling.

Think about the tree
with germ buried deep

sturdy underground
magnificent branches
outstretched strong

which have the potential to die
if the roots are deprived.

the answers are in the roots sis

Solitude

I'm most afraid to sit alone with myself
in solitude.

To feel the pain of the hunger in my belly
and not know how to fill it.

The Box

Papa Joe Smith
was listed as mulatto
on the census
sometime after 1876.

According to family gossip,
one indentured servant from
England
and a former slave from
Mississippi
had a child with light skin.

That child had more children
with mocha eyes and hues
eyes which were mixed with
brown and blue
and hair thick but straight or in
curly cues.

Most ended up in Arkansas
where they set up a sacred place
to continue cultivating from the
earth
the things they'd learned to do
as slaves.

Tending to their very own fields

the sun shone on them
and similar to the limbs of
cotton vines
generations returned to their
umber skin.

On the other side,
some dreamed beyond
separation
and trekked out west
never to be heard from again.

Living secret lives but
lives where their bodies were
away
from the smog of the South and
lungs
which could breathe
in the Pacific Coast breeze.
I wonder if
when
Papa Joe Smith
checked off that box,
he realized the power
of generational privilege
the choice (for some)
which lied in that
pen.

Dandelion Clocks

May my wishes of gratitude
take short flight
from my breath
to the grounds of Parsons.
May they plant pieces of me
in this beautiful place.
For when I become an ancestor,
I pray some child
finds solace in my shade.

The Longest Couch in the World

bocas await boleros
mischief lingers with men,
they sip rum for fun and fury
while women return or pass by coyly
and breeze gives relief and peace
along the Malecon
where
potential lovers meet

The White Magnolias

The lessons of fragrant aromas,
the haunting white magnolias.
Sometimes sweet and sometimes sour.
To those of us with "wide set noses"
a powerful cancerous odor.

Those of us whose ancestors
sacrificed strange fruit skin.
To hang for entertainment,
near magnificent, majestic,
waning, and supple flowers.

A "home" many of us refuse to return to.
Jim Crow horror stories
of wrong turns down winding dirt roads.
Lined with magnificent, majestic,
waning, and supple flowers.

We buy them in bouquets.
Place them in vases
honoring those who couldn't escape...
The lessons of fragrant aromas,
the sweet white magnolias.

There's no slander in truth...

Libéria

Ancestors speak
to me in my sleep;
I am their wildest dreams.

At times, I feel like a refugee
but without a country to return to
without a home to miss.

Stanley

I bought a mint plant
the other day.
Left it on the counter
because I was too lazy to
put it away.
Overnight, I went to rest,
forgot to water it,
and noticed the leaves
starting to limp.
The plant, I decided,
wasn't dead yet,
so I moved it to the window
and proudly
named...
him Stanley.
Got a large cup of water
and accidentally
poured it all over.
The dirt started to swim
as though it might drown.
The next day
the leaves
began to turn brown.

After sunlight
shone on him,
I remembered to
pay attention
and watered it again
as a few
signs of life returned.
But toward the bottom
the little limbs,
which were the most vulnerable,
were still gray and
most certainly dead.
I was oh so sad
to see them perish.
But I cut them off,
mourning their
neglected existence,
as to not taint
the entire plant.

While regretfully snipping away,
it occurred to me
to try
an entirely new strategy.
I got out a shallow little bowl
and placed the plant inside
filling it with
water to the halfway line.
Wouldn't you know
the next day stems
started to grow!
While the tallest
and most resilient one
now turned its leaves
face up, basking in the sun.
As the rays waved
back creating embers
against its skin.

Take a lesson from my Stanley.
Sometimes,
the problem isn't right in front of
our eyes.
We can try to water it,
move it toward the sun...
Tend to it superficially
give it our attention...
But we can't truly grow
until we tend to the root.

One other thing,
my reflective
yet naive
aspiring little botanist.
You may have started this poem
smirking at the idea
of giving a plant
of all things a name.
But let that be a lesson in itself...
Sometimes, naming it
is the first step
in claiming it
before you
can take responsibility
for the environment
which cultivates your greenery.

Plants are ancestors too.

Butterflies eventually return to the cocoon for rebirth
Flowers to the root
I return to the water.

Because

I long to be as gentle as ripples,
as powerful as waves,
and as fluid as the sea.

Daughter of Yemanja

For Fred

What happens to black boys when they commit suicide?
when the thought of not being able to stand it any longer
creeps into their head and
when life has become too great a burden to bare and
when they begin to make a plan to relieve their suffering…

Who do they tell?
when the world turns their suffering away or
doesn't recognize it packaged in this way and
when trauma threatens to drown them
because they never learned to swim…

How do they cope?
when they've poured out enough Hennessey
for other black boys who will live forever and
popped enough pills to try to forget them…
because prescriptions and therapy are an elusive myth,
Mostly to them…

Where do they go?
when schools cut guidance counselors and
social workers before security guards and
their teachers who seek to close achievement gaps,
struggle with white savior complexes and…
… and everyone forgets to ask

"How are you?"
"Are you ok?"
"Do you want to talk?"
What happens to black boys when they commit suicide?
What happens to their sister?
What happens to their father?
What happens to their mother?
What happens to their brother?

Joy

A boy and his mother
stand
with cocoa skin ever rich
and feet firmly planted in the
sand.
It's jagged with broken seashells unwelcoming to little
feet
that have just learned to walk
for the first time at the
beach.
He tosses rocks into the
sound
and with every splash
the little boy laughs and claps his
hands.
He's not old enough yet to do it all
alone
his mother guides his hand
toward the water
with a gentle strength he'll never
know.

for mothers that bury their children too young and

to young children who've buried their mother

The Day You Became an Ancestor

The day you became an ancestor
something in my bones ached
as the soles of my feet
connected with the earth
and my knees began to shake.
My stomach dropped
when my phone rang
and the voice on the other side was stale.
In a solemn low tone
it delivered the untimely news
and it all felt unfair.
The elders cried both tears
of joy and despair.
Because the possibility had always
lingered in our minds
like stale fruit next to you
by hospital bed side.
But none of us prepared for the reality that
we'd soon have to say our farewells.

dedicated to Sickle Cell Warriors and the families that love them

Amethyst

I am Jasper.

Earth, grounded, always in search of wisdom.

You are Aquamarine.

Water, vast, always in search of the serene.

The connection is profound.

A spiritual enlightenment,

absorbing of essences,

clarification of minds.

Shades of amethyst.

Decolonizing Curves II

My hips
are home to lovers,
shelters for sons and daughters.
My breasts
provide their nutrients.
My ass is fat
to stabilize the weight of the world
that's been placed on my shoulders.
Yet my lips are still so soft and pink.
How is it that you can look at this body
and not see the creator of the moon and
all the stars in the universe?

The Fear

I used to be afraid of my power.

I used to swallow it whole
even when it burned my tongue.

I'd choke it down
even when it got stuck in my throat.

afraid to step into the wind,
afraid to hone the river,
afraid to harness the moon,
afraid to bury myself deep in the dirt
to be reborn.

Love Letters from Ancestors

I outgrow myself
at least twice a year,
spend many sleepless nights
because I'm unsure of where
my soul goes to rest
when I close my eyes.
I've got a voice booming
deep in the pit of my stomach
and a muse patiently
waiting on my lips.
I'm dripping in flakes of gold
yet yearning
to return to the ground.
I exist in all of
my complications,
my contradictions,
my convictions
like a love letter
from my ancestors
giving me the courage
to persist.

truth over harmony

Becoming

I've stopped
whispering soft wishes
and started
speaking out my dreams
boldly
manifesting my words
into actions
I planted the seeds
of an internal revolution
and resolved myself
to blooming
lavishly
I am
Becoming.

I look for answers in the questions you don't ask..

Bipolar: Manic

I don't know why
      I did the thing…

But I did it.

I'm swimming in the damage
      of the thing I did
but my mind can't seem to grasp it.

I don't know why
      I did the thing…

But I did it.

I'm swimming in the damage
      of the thing I did
but I'm feeling quite apathetic.

In the Sitting Room

My sitting room
is the most beautiful room in our house.
It doesn't matter that it isn't my favorite;
I keep busy
fluffing, adjusting and dusting
ensuring everything in the room
is more than adequate.

The walls are freshly coated ivory,
I painted each stroke
in a linear pattern.
I keep a canister
of paint in the garage
in case anything grows
worn or tattered.

Flowers fill vases that are scattered.
I leave the curtains wide open
during the day
to bring energy and life
into this peaceless place
as the sunflowers reach
longingly toward sun rays.

But I never sit in this room
because I find
no contentment.
I fear the white walls
will come crashing in,
suffocating everything
with disappointment.

The sunflowers will need replacing
as their spines
eventually grow limp,
while the couch is too soft
to support my worn back.
So, I keep busy,
but never sit.

My father's been yearning to talk and
I'm afraid if I sit,
he will come in.
He will tell me,
he recognizes the smell
of Bacardi gold
early in the morning.

When two people
are so similar,
conversations often catch flame.
And even though
I'm the child,
he will tell me
I'm the one to blame.

He will step out
of the sitting room
even when it's engulfed
in the eye of the fire.
The picture of us on the mantle will burn
until we are one
figure unrecognizable.

My sister has been trying
to get ahold of me
for some time
and I fear if I sit,
she will come in
though she just wants to talk and learn
I know, she has lots of expectations.

I want to tell her
how restless my soul has become
but I fear her respect
will morph into dismay.
She'll want to pray
for my forgiveness
and so I cannot share my mistakes.

As her eyes close and her head lowers
for a prayer,
I'll catch a glimpse
of us in the mirror.
Our faces so similar
but now aged, from a childhood
I worry she doesn't remember.

My mother heals as routine responsibility
and I am terrified if I sit,
she will come in.
She sees blemishes and darkness
under my brow
and she'll tell me to
drink water for my skin.

She'll comment
on my fluctuating weight
feeding me and starving me
simultaneously.
She cultivates my perfectionism
never hugging,
nor telling me she loves me.

I'll begin to see myself
bloated, flawed, and sunken
as she tries to compensate
for the balance that I lack.
When she leaves, she will make a comment
offhandedly
about how the paint is now cracked.

Once they've gone, I'll be left alone
to sit with myself.
I'll become lost in the illusion,
and unable to maintain my will.
The walls once regal ivory
will become so desperate for my attention
they will chip and turn to eggshell.

This state of being is filled with darkness
and now, the welcoming shades
will have to come down.
The sunflowers with their
resilient and joyous spines
will have no choice but
to wilt and turn brown.

I mustn't sit, I tell myself as I walk around
in my matching white outfit.
This is hard work to maintain… But I must smile
until my gums bleed
and on the carpet,
they will leave behind
a discreet pink stain.

Diary of an oxygen mask…

Feel free to fill in the page when you feel like you can't breathe.

Fleeting Freedom

I move on from things quickly
my follow through has always shown
a lack of commitment
and that goes for people too...
Including you,
when you say,
I seem free spirited
like the kind of girl that loves trees
I think....
I do love trees but
I grew up in the city so
I smoke more trees than I hug
and I let my spirit run wild, yea
and I'm pretty sure that's
what you mean.... and
I'm pretty sure that's
what attracted you to me
but at some point
you'll probably begin to ask yourself things like...
"Will she always be this wild?"
"Will she ever settle down?"
And the yes, (to the first) may drive you crazy.
And the no (to the last) will definitely drive you away.
But baby, I'm exhausted
and I've fought so hard not to change
in that way...
Masculinity is tricky
in that way...

Jazz Tempo

Un

Holding out hope.
The tempo matches
the pace of thoughts and emotions.
Bitterness of the initial sips
bite at my lips
like all the words building up
as each minute ticks
by.
My sips get quicker
as the minutes move faster
and my frustration grows
almost unbearable.
Ponderings of worth.
Still,
Holding out hope.

Deux

Raspy voices wrap my throat.
Familiar faces join,
Offering consolation.
Giving reason, giving libation, giving distraction.
They don't know you at all.
Neither do I.
The sips grow less spiteful.
More warm.
Funny faces smile coyly perhaps also wondering.
Pondering.
What could be.
They don't know that tonight belongs to you.
I laugh.
Still,
Raspy voices wrap my throat.

Trois

The beauty and aggression in uncertainty.
Almost forgotten now
as minutes now blend together.
Passing without conscious keeping track.
I watch as the world seems to
make their bed for the night.
Filled with regret for my own disposition.
Around me voices, music, movement fill the air
giving way to my presence.
Filled with thoughts
I can't turn off.
I try to purge the bitterness
but I'm encapsulated.
Still,
The beauty and aggression in uncertainty.

He wouldn't let me
undress his soul.
But I still saw the beauty
he tried to hide.
Even now I wonder why
he hid it from me.

Vulnerability

Sagitário

I have lots of demons.
He kisses each one gently.
But not to fix me.
He loves me so tenderly.
It teaches me
to be softer with myself...

Long Distance Relationship

He went to bed feeling resolve
I, turmoil.
I wondered how we could sleep in the same space
but be miles and miles apart.

A Love Letter

When I was a sixteen-year-old girl thinking about how to have safe sex I found myself with almost nowhere to go.

I didn't want to go to my parents because I was scared that they wouldn't understand. That they would judge me or scorn me creating unhealthy ideas about sex.

I didn't want to go to my school nurse because I feared she would tell my parents. I also feared she would preach abstinence and I was in search of information.

I didn't want to go to my doctor because he might also tell my parents. But also he was "a he" and I felt too ashamed to describe my needs to a grown man.

I didn't want to go to my friends because I feared they would give me ill advice. I feared they might tell other people and I would be deemed as a slut.

I don't know how and I don't know why but I ended up at planned parenthood. A nervous teenager who had taken the bus thirty minutes to get there. Upon checking in, I was taken to the back of the clinic where I described my needs to the doctor.

"I want to know how to have safe sex." I said shyly. The female doctor, without hesitation, gave me more information then I could've imagined. We talked about sex and we talked about emotionally safe sex. We talked about my body and the ways to be in tune with it.

We talked about birth control, but not for preventing pregnancy; for my irregular period which caused me a lot of pain. I didn't even know I could regulate it. I left that conversation feeling empowered.

Empowered to advocate for my needs in a relationship.
Empowered with knowledge of how to keep myself safe.
Empowered to be and stay in tune with my body.

Thank you.
Sincerely,
A thirty something mother to be...

Pretty

Being a woman
isn't pretty.
This is sleeves rolled,
hands callused,
arms bruised
but still looking effortless
type work.
This is home after a 12hr shift,
sitting down
for the first time,
and releasing a sigh
so no one can hear you cry,
type toxins.
This is puffy eyes,
nose raw from wiping,
but still smiling
for those that depend on it
type grit.
This isn't for the dainty,
those who give up easy,
or faint of heart
type shit.
Pretending to be pretty
Is utterly exhausting so…
I quit.
I may make it look easy
deceptive in presentation
but that is the beauty of
being a Woman.

Rejection

Every item sits here almost exactly as I left it.
You can feel the tension between us
mounting in the air giving everything a thick wet stench.
I take off shoes tiptoeing into the bedroom
as my feet stick to the cool hardwood floor.

I asked you to take care of my daisies
and they're dying
as they wait for your attention to be watered.
Slumped over, limping, and holding on for dear life.
In their tear drops I can see my reflection.

As I get in bed, you barely stir to acknowledge my presence.
I kiss you, and you react naturally
so you turn the other away. You used to turn toward me,
but now my affection annoys you.
I'd cry if I wasn't used to the rejection.

I made a mess.

I made a mess.
Not the kind I'm sure I can clean up.
Broken hearts like shattered glass
are nearly impossible to put back together.

A Woman, Unchained

I've got a muse waiting
patiently on my shoulder
and an instinct on the brow
that I can't quite describe.

Wind has slapped me
in the face my entire life
and also served to hide
my tears in its strength.

I feel at home in so many places
it can be unsettling.
I am restless for nostalgia, and
tortured by my own reckoning.

Growing on the same vine
I am
dying, budding, and in full bloom
all at the same time.

I am grateful for transformations,
though the process can be draining
I am constantly evolving
which most often is hard to explain.

I am everything a woman is not supposed to be
boisterous, wild, uncontained
but I am woman
vivacious, brazen, and unchained.

If I must swallow my
    education
     for misguided
     opinion,

If I must digest my
    experience
    in solitude and
    silence,

If I must curl up
    the corners of my mouth
    into a smile and swallow the truth
    (just to please you).

Then I'd rather not be invited
(for a seat at your table).

A single seat at your table has not meant inclusivity,
and swallowing myself whole will be my defeat.

- I politely decline

Truth Over Harmony

My tongue was not made
square nor sweet for
contentment nor comfort.

The creator who sculpted me
(in her image)
has no regard for your palette.

\\

To Be Desired

He devours her essence
the energy between them
is palpable.

Eyes watch enviously
how youthful it is
to be desired.

Erotica To A Poet

Sex doesn't inspire me the way
stimulating conversations can lead down windy roads
coffee in bed on Sundays with theory
and debates which lead to kisses and kisses which lead to....
when we part, oh when we part
don't send nudes, send words
start with your favorite
tell me what it means to you so I can imagine
how it would feel to indulge you in it, speaking of it
I'll ask you what your favorite part of a woman's body is
and when you answer look deeply into my eyes and tell me
it's her mind...
the straight forwardness of your gaze
and the depth of your soul
will send butterflies down my spine
tell me about philosophers,
ones that challenge me to grapple with new concepts
ones that inspire me to...
write poetry
the kind of poetry that causes your mouth to curl up in that coy little
smile, that smile
when you realize you're my muse
and the poems I've written for you are the deepest form of my intimacy

Remember if
you want to touch me...

with your hands..

Start first
by touching me
with your heart.

Restless Yet Home

I love how your body
conforms to me in your sleep.
It contorts attempting to
take up space in all my nooks and crannies.
At a time when you lack control
over the space of your limbs,
everything in you seems
to bend toward me.
When you breath in deep,
it's like you're inhaling every fiber,
every nuance of my complicated being.
When you exhale,
all of my toxins,
all of my indiscretions...
The act is freeing
it's that type of uninhibited reaction,
that speaks to the purity of your intentions.
To just purely love me,
your need to be loved by me.
It truly inspires me
speaks to the desire in me.
To be that free
with you
in return.

Vows

Many people think that love stories are written in gigantic moments. At the start of our relationship there were many gigantic moments. Milestones filled with butterflies, excitement, and even bittersweet turmoil at times. The emotions were raw and the connection was intangible. From our first kiss to the first time we said I love you, everything felt monumental. We both knew our relationship would ultimately be momentous.

But the reason I want to marry you is not because of *that* love story, or all those gigantic moments. Ultimately those raw emotions can fade over time if they don't eventually evaporate completely. The reason I am marrying you is because of all the miniscule moments. Though often overlooked in love stories, it's these moments where I see you the clearest. It's the day to day grind and the minutes that seem to tick by slowly on lazy days where your place in my life is magnified with clarity. Sundays are the perfect day to illustrate the nuance of happiness you bring to my life. Having spent at least 250 Sundays with you, I know that I want to spend every Sunday with you.

I want to wake up next to you every Sunday morning and feel the warmth of your hands as they tickle the crevices of my arms. I want to stroke your morning glory as you scurry away coyly and out of bed. I want to hear the eggs crackling on the stove, as I anticipate your companionship. And every Sunday afternoon, I want our feet to intertwine as we make our plans for the following day. I want to see that hesitant begrudging look on your face as I drag you on one of my spontaneous adventures. And as we get ready for bed I want to kiss you softly on your lips and let you feel all the love pouring out of me. I want to pour love into you every day of our marriage on Sundays, on hard days, on good days.

I want you to know now that I can pour all of this love out of me because of you, and I hope you never forget that I want you to know that, you make all the mundane things in life extraordinary. You make all the mundane things fun, you make them memorable, and it makes my life worth living to the fullest. In these miniscule moments, I can feel the depth of how much you love me. And I can only begin to grasp how important it is for you to provide me with loyalty, commitment, stability, support, and friendship.

So knowing that I am imperfect,
but also recognizing that you
already love every part of me;
Here are some things I can commit to
because of you,

I can commit my body only to yours
after all I was made from your rib
connecting us at our core.
I can commit to always coming home
though my wanderlust may lead me astray
and I value my time alone.
I can commit to maintaining the integrity
with moral uprightness choosing to always
operate in the spirit of fidelity.
I can commit to respecting who you are
who you will be, who you are becoming,
who I am becoming will never be too far.
I can commit to basking in your accomplishments,
I promise to live in them with excitement full of decadence.
I can commit to watching you flourish
and hope that I may harvest some of your excellence.
I can commit to watching you grow from your mistakes,
we will make mistakes together, but we will never break
because of you.

As we change and grow and as our family expands, Sundays will inevitably change. There
will undoubtedly be good and bad times. But I know there is no one else in this world other
than you that I want to spend my days with. Because you are everything. The moon. The sun.
All the stars in the sky. You are the infinity. You are never ending. You are the man beyond
anything I could dream.

Sins of the Secular

I've been both prayer warrior and condemned sinner;
blameful Eve
and
innocent Maria.
The Virgin of Guadalupe
has found me
in sketchy dive bars
at closing time
and in church pews
on early Sundays
worshipping by my mother's side.

Beyond the Brick

I long to be
beyond the brick
where the sirens
and metropolitan violence
do not exist
where "excuse me"
cannot interrupt internal bliss
where you can embrace
sounds
birds chirping
waves rippling
and

silence …

take notes
from the sun
how it
rises and shines
while the world
creates constraints
called time
to simply revolve
around it

never shy away from your shine sis

The Whisperings of the Wilting

I've come to realize
that I am a living thing
with both a fall and a spring.

Some of us forget
to embrace
the wilting.

Death and decay
a sign;
rebirth is on its way.

A signal to the universe
that we are making space
for new things to flourish.

Author's Biography

The poems in this book once lived in a journal. They were collected over a decade and hidden away, they were streams of consciousness and musings Lyn wrote when she felt the world was moving around her while she stood still. Though Lyn had been writing since elementary and studied poetry in college during a semester abroad, she never considered herself a poet. She used poetry to talk about the trauma of addiction, the difficulties of achieving mental wellness, and fear. Maybe it was fear that kept her from being raw, emotional, and vulnerable with people.

But this year she decided to lean into fear and began posting her work on social media, developing a community of readers and other poets (for whom she is eternally grateful). She started on Instagram as an anonymous poet, which gave her the confidence to explore the deepest recesses of her personality. She often found herself reeling, and sharing poetry became therapeutic. More and more people began to share how her poems had resonated with them and it gave her the courage to put this collection together.

Lyn finds inspiration in the concepts of duality and femininity. She's come to believe that everyone's existence is along spectrums, which causes us to find ourselves wedged between contradictions - and that accepting this duality causes personal evolution, as well as resolve in the face of the adversity that we all face. She decided to share this collection specifically because women are not always afforded the grace of being wedged in contradictions. She wanted to share stories with her former self, as affirmations that women are divinely wild regardless of the restrictions society places upon them as they step into new roles such as adult, wife, or mother.

The whisperings represent ancestors. From 2011 she began collecting family documents to solve generational mysteries and answer the ever-present question, "what are you?" The quest at times revealing even more questions than answers. She has learned that placing yourself in space, time, and history is an empowering journey of self-actualization. Ancestors pass on wisdom to us by whispering to our instincts and guiding our third eye. These whisperings sit deep within our chests and often erupt as a spirit of wildness or a contentment with wilting. Lyn's world travels have taught her to listen to ancestors as they are always whispering us toward our divine purpose.

Art has always been a calling to Lyn. As an artist Lyn has learned to express herself through different mediums. Before poetry, her loves were music and dance. She performed as a dancer for many years before publishing undergraduate academic research on dance education. Her current focus is on African diasporic dance as she has been dancing salsa and samba for over ten years. She has been published in 10 print publications, featured in many digital publications, and appeared on numerous podcasts. She runs a poetry book club called @canwediscusspoetry and is currently helping to curate an anthology with Wide Eyes Publishing that focuses on empowering women through poetry. Outside of her art, Lyn is an educator and trains new teachers.

132

Made in the
USA
Columbia, SC